A Desert Habitat

Introducing Habitats

Kelley MacAulay and Bobbie Kalman

Crabtree Publishing Company

www.crabtreebooks.com

Created by Bobbie Kalman

Dedicated by Heather Fitzpatrick
For my dear friends Mike and Steve — Congratulations!

Editor-in-Chief
Bobbie Kalman

Writing team
Kelley MacAulay
Bobbie Kalman

Substantive editor
Kathryn Smithyman

Editors
Molly Aloian
Michael Hodge
Rebecca Sjonger

Design
Katherine Kantor
Samantha Crabtree
(cover and series logo)

Production coordinator
Heather Fitzpatrick

Photo research
Crystal Foxton

Special thanks to
Jack Pickett and Karen Van Atte

Illustrations
Barbara Bedell: pages 17, 32 (top left and bottom right)
Katherine Kantor: pages 15, 32 (bottom left)

Photographs
Photo Researchers Inc.: Craig K. Lorenz: page 20 (right);
    Tom McHugh: page 23
Visuals Unlimited: Jim Merli: page 25
© Rich Wagner/WildNaturePhotos: page 29
Other images by Corbis, Corel, Digital Stock, Digital Vision, and Photodisc

Library and Archives Canada Cataloguing in Publication

MacAulay, Kelley
    A desert habitat / Kelley MacAulay & Bobbie Kalman.
(Introducing habitats)
Includes index.
ISBN-13: 978-0-7787-2950-1 (bound)
ISBN-10: 0-7787-2950-8 (bound)
ISBN-13: 978-0-7787-2978-5 (pbk.)
ISBN-10: 0-7787-2978-8 (pbk.)
    1. Desert ecology--Juvenile literature. I. Kalman, Bobbie, date.
II. Title. III. Series.

QH541.5.D4M33 2006   j577.54   C2006-904075-3

Library of Congress Cataloging-in-Publication Data

MacAulay, Kelley.
    A desert habitat / Kelley MacAulay & Bobbie Kalman.
      p. cm. -- (Introducing habitats)
    Includes index.
    ISBN-13: 978-0-7787-2950-1 (rlb)
    ISBN-10: 0-7787-2950-8 (rlb)
    ISBN-13: 978-0-7787-2978-5 (pb)
    ISBN-10: 0-7787-2978-8 (pb)
    1. Desert ecology--Juvenile literature. I. Kalman, Bobbie. II. Title.
    QH541.5.D4M33 2007
    577.54--dc22
                                        2006018058

Crabtree Publishing Company

www.crabtreebooks.com   1-800-387-7650

Published in Canada
Crabtree Publishing
616 Welland Ave.
St. Catharines, ON
L2M 5V6

Published in the United States
Crabtree Publishing
PMB16A
350 Fifth Ave., Suite 3308
New York, NY 10118

Published in the United Kingdom
Crabtree Publishing
White Cross Mills
High Town, Lancaster
LA1 4XS

Published in Australia
Crabtree Publishing
386 Mt. Alexander Rd.
Ascot Vale (Melbourne)
VIC 3032

Contents

What is a habitat?

A **habitat** is a place in nature. Plants live in habitats. Animals live in habitats, too. Some animals make homes in habitats.

Living and non-living things

There are **living things** in habitats. Plants and animals are living things. There are also **non-living things** in habitats. Rocks, water, and dirt are non-living things.

Everything they need

Plants and animals need air, water, and food to stay alive. Plants and animals find the things they need in their habitats. This iguana found some food to eat. It is eating a cactus.

A habitat home

Some animals have homes.

Their homes are in their habitats.

This baby coyote's home is a hole.

The coyote sleeps in the hole.

Desert habitats

Deserts are habitats. Desert habitats are very hot and dry. Deserts can be flat or hilly. Some deserts are mainly sand. Camels live in sandy deserts.

The Sonoran Desert

This book is about the Sonoran Desert. The Sonoran Desert is in the southern United States. It is also in northern Mexico. Plants grow in the Sonoran Desert. Many animals also live there. This cottontail rabbit lives in the Sonoran Desert.

Desert weather

The weather in the Sonoran Desert is very hot or very cold. During the day, the weather is very hot. At night, the weather is very cold. It does not rain much in the desert. The desert is very dry.

Rainy days

In the Sonoran Desert, it rains in the spring. It also rains at the end of summer. Plants grow when it rains. Many flowers bloom.

Sonoran Desert plants

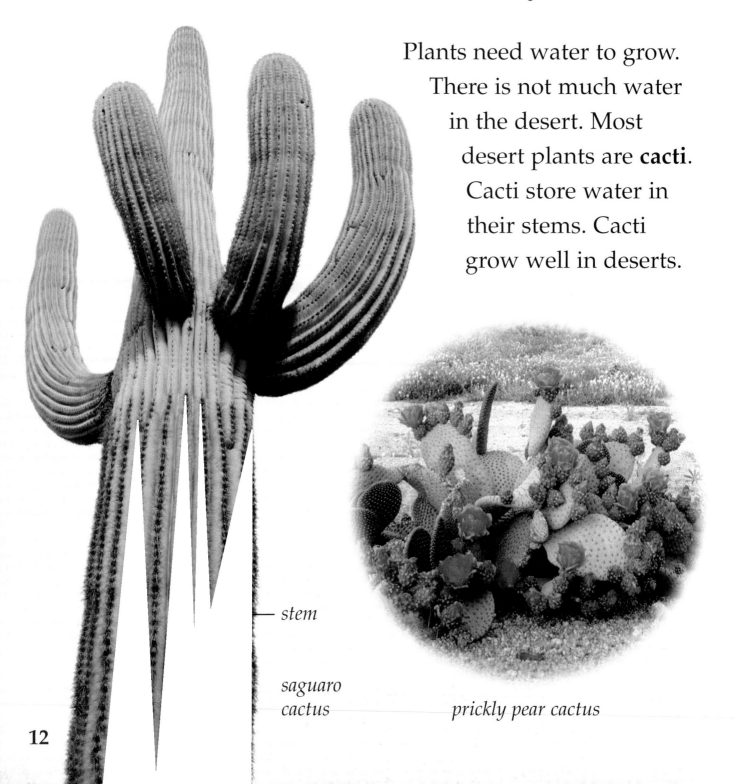

Plants need water to grow. There is not much water in the desert. Most desert plants are **cacti**. Cacti store water in their stems. Cacti grow well in deserts.

stem

saguaro cactus

prickly pear cactus

Flowers and fruit

Flowers grow on cacti when it rains. Fruits grow on cacti in spring. Some animals eat the flowers and fruits.

fruit

flower

Plants make food

Living things need food. Plants make their own food. They make food from sunlight, air, and water. Using sunlight, air, and water to make food is called **photosynthesis**.

Taking in water

The roots of plants take in water when it rains. Desert plants have long roots. The roots grow out to the sides. Desert plants grow far away from one another. They need room to spread out their roots.

Desert animals

These animals live in the Sonoran Desert. They are suited to life in this hot habitat. The animals know how to keep cool. They know how to find food. They also know how to find homes.

desert hairy scorpion

burrowing owl

desert tortoise

rattlesnake

coyote

kit fox

gila monster

17

Food in the desert

Animals find food in the desert. Some animals eat only plants. Animals that eat only plants are called **herbivores**. This iguana is a herbivore. It is eating part of a cactus.

Eating animals

Many desert animals are **carnivores**. Carnivores eat other animals. Kit foxes are carnivores. They eat mice and birds.

Eating anything

Some Sonoran Desert animals are **omnivores**. Omnivores eat both plants and animals. Roadrunners are omnivores. This roadrunner is eating a lizard.

19

Getting energy

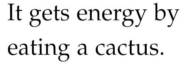
sun

All living things need **energy**. Energy helps them grow and move. Energy comes from the sun. Plants use the sun's energy to make food. Animals get energy by eating. A jackrabbit is a herbivore. It gets energy by eating a cactus.

cactus

jackrabbit

Energy for carnivores

A carnivore gets energy by eating other animals. A hawk is a carnivore. It gets energy by eating a jackrabbit.

hawks

Underground homes

Many desert animals live in homes.
Some homes are under the ground.
Underground homes are called **burrows**.
Burrowing owls live in burrows.
They put soft grass in their homes.
They sleep on the grass.

Cool inside

Animals must keep cool in the desert. Burrows are cool homes. Animals keep cool in their burrows. This kangaroo rat is inside its burrow.

Homes above the ground

Some desert animals live above the ground. They often make homes in tall cacti. These homes are called **nests**. The animals are safe in their high nests. Animals on the ground cannot reach them. This great horned owl is safe in its nest.

Wandering around

Other animals do not make homes.
They wander from place to place.
They find cool places to rest.
These collard peccaries are
sleeping under a cactus.
They stay cool in the shade.

tarantula

Night life

Some animals leave their homes only at night. Night time is cool in the desert. The animals sleep during the day, while it is hot. Tarantulas and gila monsters come out at night.

gila monster

Food in the dark

Coyotes search for food at night. They can smell food in the dark. Coyotes often howl at night!

Long sleeps

Summer is the hottest time of year in the desert. Some desert animals sleep through summer. They sleep in cool underground homes. Desert tortoises sleep through summer.

Less energy

Animals that sleep through summer do not wake up often. They use less energy while they sleep. Sleeping animals do not need to eat or drink often. This toad is burying itself in sand. It will sleep through summer under the ground.

Staying safe

Desert animals need to stay safe from other animals. They stay safe in different ways. A rattlesnake has a **rattle** on its tail. When a rattlesnake shakes its tail, the rattle makes noise. The noise scares away other animals.

rattle

Hard to see

These squirrels have brown bodies.
Desert sand is also brown. The squirrels
stay safe because their color hides them.
It is hard for other animals to see the
squirrels on the sand.

Words to know and Index

animals
pages 4, 5, 6, 7, 9,
13, 16-17, 18, 19, 20,
21, 22, 23, 24, 25,
26, 28, 29, 30, 31

deserts
pages 8, 9, 10, 11,
12, 15, 16, 18, 19, 22,
23, 24, 26, 28, 30, 31

energy
pages 20-21, 29

food
pages 6, 14, 16,
18-19, 20, 27, 29

habitats
pages 4, 5, 6, 7, 8, 16

homes
pages 4, 7, 16, 22-25,
26, 28

plants
pages 4, 5, 6, 9, 11,
12-13, 14, 15, 18,
19, 20,

sleep
pages 7, 22, 25, 26,
28-29

Other index words
carnivores 19, 21
herbivores 18, 20
living things 5, 14, 20
non-living things 5
omnivores 19
photosynthesis 14
water 5, 6, 12, 14, 15, 29

1 2 3 4 5 6 7 8 9 0 Printed in the U.S.A. 5 4 3 2 1 0 9 8 7 6